LET
HER
KNOW
YOU
Love
HER

Bill Farrel

HARVEST HOUSE PUBLISHERS
Eugene, Oregon 97402

Verses marked NIV are taken from the Holy Bible, New International Version ®, Copyright © 1973, 1978, 1984 by the International Bible Society. Used by permission of Zondervan Publishing House. The "NIV" and "New International Version" trademarks are registered in the United States Patent and Trademark Office by International Bible Society.

Cover design by Koechel Peterson and Associates, Minneapolis, Minnesota

Let Her Know You Love Her

Copyright 1998 by Bill Farrel
Published by Harvest House Publishers
Eugene, Oregon 97402

Library of Congress Cataloging-in-Publication Data

Farrel, Bill, 1959–
    Let her know you love her / Bill Farrel.
        p.   cm.
    ISBN 1-56507-687-7
    1. Marriage.   2. Communication in marriage.
    3. Marriage—Religious aspects—Christianity.   I. Title.
HQ734.F26   1998
306.81—DC21   97-5185
                                                                    CIP

Printed in the United States of America.

98 99 00 01 02 03 04 / BP / 10 9 8 7 6 5 4 3 2 1

To Pam, my Angel

You have taken me to heights I never knew existed.
You have shown me adventures I never dreamed of.
In falling in love with you, I have found myself.

Contents

1

Men Are Like Waffles, Women Are Like Spaghetti

For two days, I have been
asking myself every moment if such
happiness is not a dream.

—VICTOR HUGO

*G*uys, have you been wondering why women are so hard to figure out? Have you been thinking about how much simpler life would be if your wife thought the same way you do? Well, *it will never happen . . .* so each of us had better get about the business of figuring out how to most effectively encourage and love the woman he has chosen to live with.

It has been said that men and women are different in every way, but that is not exactly true. You and your wife are actually alike in many areas. You probably have the same spiritual values, share many of the same preferences in style and taste, come from the same socio-economic background, and share similar approaches to decision-making. But when

---

✦ *How to Pick Up Your Wife:* So, what are you doing for the next twenty or thirty years?

Encouraging Words

Walk hand in hand with your lover in a public place and tell her how proud you are to be seen with her.

———※———

After 21 years of marriage, we were out walking together holding hands at the fair. He turned to me and said, "I love being out in public with you."

—Cindy Terrell, Bakersfield

it comes to the way you think through life, you are radically different.

The way I see it, *Men are like waffles and women are like spaghetti.* Let's deal with us guys first. If you look at a waffle, you see a lot of individual boxes with walls between them. Each box is separate and does not interact with the other boxes. We deal with life as if there were a waffle in our brain. We take one issue and put it in a box. We take the next issue and put it in another box. If we could do an MRI on our thinking, it would look just like a waffle—little boxes, each holding one area of life. We deal with one thing at time and one thing only. When we are fishing, we are fishing. When we are at work, we are at work. When we are doing yard work, we are doing yard work. And when we are having sex with our wives, we are thinking ONLY about sex.

Our wives, on the other hand, approach life like spaghetti. If you look at a plate of spaghetti, you immediately notice that everything is touching everything else. That is the way women process life. They connect everything! They have this incredible ability to deal with multiple things at the same time.

Since it is impossible to fix everything and have it all under control at once, our wives process life by connecting to everything emotionally.

My wife will travel through a conversation, emotionally connecting with each thing on her mind until she has "felt" something about each issue in her life. She may experience positive emotions like sentimentality, joy, and enthusiasm or she may experience negative emotions like anger, depression, or frustration, but the key for her is *to experience some emotion*. Once she has emotionally connected with each issue in her life, she will relax and begin to thoroughly enjoy the people around her.

The problem with this disparity is the tension it causes in our marriages. For example, your wife begins a conversation with you. You think the talk is about *one* issue. About the time you start offering a solution to the problem, she

The Gift of Love

Give your wife a gift arranged among a favorite dessert. On the plate put a small card that says, "It is so sweet to be married to you."

—⚬—

My husband proposed to me at a restaurant. The waitress brought dessert right after he asked me to marry him. The covered silver platter contained my engagement ring on a bed of roses. He has since had "dessert" delivered like that on several anniversaries.

Marlene Aten, Paso Robles

Building Anticipation

Choose a day, other than your anniversary and her birthday, to commemorate your love for your wife. It could be the day of your first kiss, your first date, Valentine's Day, or a day that is uniquely meaningful to you. Celebrate this day every year with a special dinner where you lavish her with your attention. Your wife will eagerly await this dinner each year, and you will enthusiastically enjoy dessert.

—ᴧᴧ—

My husband belongs to a small group of men who have started a Valentine's tradition. They fix us wives a special dinner, do the dishes, and always plan a special gift. Last year it was a basket with scented candles, oils, and soaps, I can't wait until next year!

Kim Sonoda, Oceanside

changes the subject. You listen and discover the next problem she wants to talk about. You offer more insightful answers, and your wife changes the subject again. You grow increasingly frustrated with the conversation because you aren't sure what your wife is doing. Is she deliberately trying to evade your help, or is she just an irrational, unreasonable person? Or maybe it's you. You begin thinking, "Maybe I'm a conversational idiot, or perhaps I don't know how to listen, but I just don't get it."

Our wives will change subjects in conversation at will as they connect all the pieces of life together. It is as if they are traveling around a plate of spaghetti, switching directions each time two noodles intersect. Pam and I had a conversation recently that sounded like this:

"Sweetheart," my wife began, "did you work out at the gym today?"

"No, I didn't," I replied, "I was going to on my lunch break, but I got so wrapped up in work that I just ate at my desk."

"Oh, well," she said "I was thinking about you today as I drove past the gym, so I went to the store and bought some of your favorite soup. You know, that really good clam chowder."

"So we're having soup for dinner?"

"Yeah. I haven't made it yet because I was helping the kids with their homework. I thought it would be great though because it reminded me of when we were just dating and couldn't afford much. We ate a lot of clam chowder then."

"I remember" I responded, reflecting on those days, "but we had to settle for the cheap stuff. I didn't think clam chowder would ever taste good again after the gallons of it we had to eat in those first few years."

"You don't want soup for dinner?" There was a note of regret in her voice.

Just the Two of Us

Go on a Car Rally. Plan a date where you do everything in your car. Take a driving tour of the interesting sights in your city. Go to a drive-through restaurant that you don't usually frequent. Enjoy a drive-in movie together.

"I'm not saying that, honey. I was just making a comment."

"Well if you want something else, that's okay. I just
thought soup would be nice."

"Soup is fine, dear."

"Okay," she sighed. "Just thinking about dinner reminds
me of what a good marriage we have. We sure have been
through a lot together in these 10 years."

"It seems like the hard times have just pulled us closer
together. You have been a wonderful wife. You know, thinking about soup for dinner is kind of getting me in the mood."

"I wish everyone had as good a marriage as we have. Did you
hear how Paul and Beth are doing? I heard they had another big
fight. I hope they figure out a way to stay together."

"Paul and Beth. Do I know them?"

"You know, they are the neighbors of John and Susan we
met at Peter's baseball game. I wanted us to spend time with

them because Beth knows Jane who is going to be in charge of the Parent Teacher Association next year at Janet's school. I told you we were going to try and get together with them soon."

I just sat staring for a minute before asking, "How did you do that?"

"Do what?"

"How did you get all those names straight without slowing down?"

"Oh sweetheart, you are so silly." Pam laughed, then added, "Well, anyway, if Paul and Beth were to break up, it would be hard on the kids."

"Have Paul and Beth thought about how this would affect the kids? They seem like involved parents." Then, leaning back in my chair, I asked, "Why would they do this?"

A Little Extra

Temporarily decorate some part of your house with notes that express how valuable your lover is to you.

—⁓—

My fiancé, before leaving for a summer at military school, snuck into my room and left notes hidden all around. My favorite said, "You are the very best thing that has ever happened to me."

Subine Strickland

The Gift of Love

Buy a song that expresses the way you feel about your lover. Sit her down in a comfortable place and serve her a cup of her favorite tea or hot chocolate. Tell her, "This is how I feel about you," then play the song.

—⁓—

We were getting ready for a trip. I had encouraged my husband to go to bed since we were leaving early, and I wanted him rested. I packed the kids clothes, then went to the garage to load them. I opened the car door and saw a note that said, Turn on the CD and listen to the first song—I mean it. I pray that we have a good holiday. Love, Jim. The song was Amy Grant's I'm the Lucky One. I realized that night that I truly am the lucky one!

"Speaking of our kids," Pam continued, "they will all need rides to their games on Saturday. Do you think you will be able to go?"

Conversations like these can leave your head spinning. Just about the time you think you know what your wife is talking about, she switches gears and moves on to something else. As you observe her skills, she appears to think that all the various topics are somehow linked to one another, but for you it is a challenge to stay tuned in.

When your wife does this, are you tempted to stop her from talking and focus her on *one* of the issues she has brought up? When you lead the conversation, does your wife try to make you more sensitive as she helps you integrate all the other issues of your life with the issue you want to talk about? If you have ever been through this common wrestling match of married couples, then you know how futile it is to attempt to change the way the other communicates. It is as if you have pulled out a fork and knife and you are attempting to take the plate of spaghetti and organize it into little squares that will transform your wife into a waffle, while your wife is using her knife to break down the walls of the waffle and turn you into a plate of spaghetti! This only serves to frustrate both of you and stall the growth of your relationship.

I see this in action with Pam every time I get a day off. On those days, I like to leave work and get lost in some hobby or project. For me, days off are good days for fishing, yard work, and washing the cars. For Pam, these are good days for comparing calendars, planning vacations, shopping together, and reviewing goals. She likes this approach because it enables her to connect her life together. I don't like it because it forces me to jump boxes quickly in order to keep up with her.

Pam will come bouncing into the kitchen on one of these precious days and ask, "What are you doing today? Can we go over our calendars?"

These words send chills up and down my spine unlike anything else in our relationship. But, because I love Pam like no one else, I usually give it a try. I like the way she responds when we successfully navigate the organization of our schedules—she becomes soft and flirty. She wants to spend time with me and usually is interested in being intimate. But if I'm not ready for a spaghetti conversation, the results can be disastrous. About the time she is feeling like

Let Her Know You Love Her

Without your wife knowing, put a page in your personal organizer for taking notes on every date you and your wife share for a year. Put a box in your office where you save keepsakes from each of those dates. On your anniversary, go through the box with your wife and talk about the things you wrote down about each date.

—⚡—

Martin is a bit more sentimental than I and he saved EVERYTHING from our dates. After dating for six years, he collected quite a bit of stuff! On the day of our engagement, that pile of information came in handy. Martin took me to the museum of our very first date, the beach where we first kissed, and so on. He proposed on the beach where our first kiss was shared. It meant a great deal to me that he remembered such details.

the spaghetti sauce is warm, I'm feeling like she is putting it on my waffle.

"What are you doing this week?" she asks innocently. This question works fine, because I can stand in the schedule box and focus on the activities of my week. But invariably my answer to this one question leads to another.

"What would you like to do for vacation this year?" Pam introduces, as she is reminded that we haven't made any reservations yet. I now move one foot into the vacation box to deal with this request, but leave one foot in the schedule box because I know we are not done with that one yet. We dream about what we would like to do this year and come up with some fun ideas until she pushes for a decision.

"We need to decide. Where would you most like to go?" Now I stretch to put one hand in the decision-making box, knowing that Pam will judge my enthusiasm about being with her based on my choice. If I want to go camping and save money for a house project, I run the risk of giving the impression that the house is more important than Pam. On the other hand, if I want to rent a houseboat and jet skis, she might think I am being selfish and that I just want to have my kind of fun. I must use discernment that will open up her heart, so I try to stretch my other hand to reach the romance box to provide my vacation recommendation with the proper balance. At this point I am usually doing all right, but Pam doesn't stop here. She almost always opens another box because she can do so with ease.

"We also need to decide when we are taking the boys shopping for school." At this point I start to become over-whelmed, but I try not to show it. I am getting too many boxes open, and I'm having to make more decisions than I

The Great Escape

Look in the entertainment section of the newspaper in the city closest to you. Find a jazz concert (or your favorite music) coming soon. Make reservations at a hotel close by. Plan a nice dinner and an evening at the concert, followed by a relaxing night's sleep. Send her a note in the mail that says, "Being with you is the greatest jazz of my life."

From Pam's Heart

Endearing names, we women love them. Early in our relationship Bill began calling me *Angel* because he felt like ours was a match made in heaven. No one else calls me *Angel*. That is Bill's lover's name. I love writing my love letters to him or sending sultry cards to the office and signing them *Angel*. I even love boldly leaving post-it notes for him all over the house and office signed *Your Angel*. Being Bill's *Angel* sets me apart. No other women is his lover. No other women can demand to be put through immediately on the phone or march straight into his office—only his *Angel*. Everytime he says, *Angel*, even if it is tagged on to a request, I feel special, set apart from all other women in the world.

am in the mood to make. But by this time in the conversation Pam is on a roll, feeling like her plate of spaghetti is coming together nicely. She brings up the visit of her mom, the party we're having at our house in three weeks, the business trip she needs to start planning for next month, then wants to know when I am going to call my brother. Sometimes I just throw my hands into the air and declare, "You win!"

The only way for me to navigate Pam's need for emotional connection is to prepare for the planning encounters and then let her lead the conversation. I write into my calendar the days I am going to plan with Pam. This gives me time to psyche up for the event and get myself in the right frame of mind to journey through life with my wife. I find when I do this, I am amazed at Pam's ability to juggle the balls of our life. I am equally amazed at how irritated I can get by this same ability when I am in extreme waffle mode.

The problem is not that we are different, but that we don't know how to handle our differences. Too often we expect each other to act like the opposite sex. We expect our wives to think like men, and our wives expect their husbands to think like women. This is the equivalent of pouring spaghetti sauce on waffles and pancake syrup on spaghetti.

Use Your Imagination

Give someone else a monetary reward for noticing your wife's beauty or value. Make sure she knows you have done this as an announcement of your love for her.

—✺—

A homeless man was begging money off my friend, Jim, who was taking his wife out to dinner to patch things up with her and try to make her feel special. Jim said to the panhandler, "Sorry, I don't have any money to give you."

The homeless man looked at Jim's beautiful wife and said, "Whoa, if I had a wife who looked like that, I'd be broke too!"

As they sat down in the nearby restaurant, Jim looked his wife in the eyes and told her the homeless man was right about her being gorgeous.

Jim then got out of his seat, went back outside, and gave the man twenty dollars. "Hey," Jim added, "I owe you a lot more than this, but I hope this helps."

—Bill Farrel

When you look at it this way, it is not very attractive. I for one do not want to eat maple flavored spaghetti, nor am I interested in waffles marinara. In the same way, I do not want to be married to another me. I got married because I was not content to live with just me. I wanted more variety and another perspective that would fill my gaps. Why would I later *complain* that the different perspective is actually different?

This book is my attempt to help guys figure out the implications of having a wife that is like spaghetti when we face life like a waffle. As we journey together through the maze of encouraging our wives, I hope you find ideas and principles to enrich your relationship. Maybe as we explore this mystery together you can avoid the pitfalls and discover the adventure of a happy and fulfilled marriage, as you let her know you love her.

2

I Will Be
Your Mirror

Like a lily among the thorns
is my darling among the maidens.
All beautiful you are, my darling,
there is no flaw in you.

—KING SOLOMON TO HIS BRIDE

I was on my December honeymoon having an incredible time. Here I was in a cozy Lake Tahoe mountain resort, all alone with the woman of my dreams. I had decided as a young man to wait to have sex until my wedding night, so the thought of being alone with Pam in a hotel room was pretty exciting. I was prepared to thoroughly enjoy our special time!

On the fourth morning of the honeymoon I was lying in bed thinking about what an awesome thing marriage was. It was almost like I was living a dream. I had time off from the pressures of work, and the day-to-day responsibilities of life seemed so far away. I had been introduced to the wonders of intimacy between a man and woman, and we had a good start on marriage.

❧ *How to Pick Up Your Wife:* You've been running through my mind all day long.

Memories

Write your loved one a note that reminds her, and you, of the good times you have had together.

—ɷ—

My husband and I have been married for 47 years. He has the habit of sending cards for my birthday and our anniversary. For the past two years, he has written inside the card, "I'm falling in love with you all over again."

Marian McBride, Whittier

Just the two of us

Plan a date based on your wife's name. Choose an activity for each letter in her name, or better yet, choose an activity for each letter in your name for her. For instance, I could take Pam on a date where we **P**lan our next vacation together, go to an **Ar**t store and talk about what we like and don't like, then have a **M**eal at her favorite restaurant.

As I was lying there thinking about what a lucky guy I was, I noticed Pam stepping out of the shower. At this, my thoughts were overcome with amazement. I was not only in a mountain resort having a great vacation, but I was in a hotel room with a beautiful naked woman standing in front of me . . . and it was right! God smiled on this and said it was good. I could gaze at this marvelous creation standing before me. I was free to take in the sights with all the confidence and joy of a kid opening Christmas presents. I was lost in the thought that God did a good job creating this male-female thing.

Then, right before my eyes, the scene started to change. My wife stood in front of the mirror combing her hair and verbally criticizing her body from head to toe. Nothing seemed right to her. Her hair was the wrong color. Her skin wasn't smooth enough. Her breasts weren't the right size. Her legs were too short.

I *hate* it when women do this. Just about the time you figure life can't get any better, it takes a frustrating turn. The woman of your dreams becomes an emotional nightmare. Your personal vision of beauty fades as the fog of insecurity rolls in and blocks your view. Your plans of a free flowing, easygoing relationship with your wife turns into a dance that leaves you feeling like you have two left feet. I couldn't believe this was happening to me. My wife's happiness was important to me, but I was angry that her insecurity was stealing my pleasure.

I knew I had to take drastic measures. I wanted to jump out of bed and set her straight by forcing her to like herself. I thought about getting angry with her and telling her to stop, but I figured that would work about as well as trying to fix a computer with a hammer. Then I thought about going for a walk to get away from this most unwelcome soliloquy,

The Great Escape

Get a copy of the yellow pages from the mountain resort closest to your home and choose a cottage rental for a cozy getaway. Call the visitor's bureau to locate a company that provides carriage rides. After a nice dinner, take a carriage ride under the moonlight, and then head to your private cottage for hot chocolate and a blazing fire to spark your love.

but I realized the scenery outside was not nearly as good as the scenery inside this room.

Suddenly a brainstorm hit me. I walked over to Pam as she was brushing her hair and took the brush out of her hands. I then turned her toward me and made her look at me rather than the mirror. I softly cradled her face in my hands, gazed into her eyes and said,

> Pam, from now on *I* will be your mirror. Anytime you need to know how beautiful you are, you come to me and I will reflect back to you the beautiful and valuable woman God has made you. And Pam, if I have to throw away every mirror in our house to get you to believe me, I will. From now on, I will be your mirror.

Pam's response made it obvious I had made a strategic maneuver. It was as if we fell in love all over again. In a moment, her heart became soft and her eyes brightened. The pride welled up in my heart as I realized I had hit the target dead center. The atmosphere in our relationship was suddenly brighter and intimacy was easier to achieve. It

Just the Two of Us

Impress her with a spring flower date. Buy her a dozen roses to begin the date. Pack a picnic lunch and take her to a place where the flowers are blooming. While you enjoy the meal, talk about the time when you first knew you were in love with her. Buy a card for her that says, "My life has been more colorful since our love blossomed."

Talking It Over

Questions for you: Do you feel most respected when your wife agrees with you? your wife notices an accomplishment in your life? your wife asks your advice for a decision she has to make? your wife compliments your good looks? your wife cheerfully gives you free time?

Questions for her: What areas of life do you find it easiest to succeed in?

What types of conversations between us make you feel good about yourself?

What picture comes to mind when you think about our wedding day?

seemed to me that I had been able to open the door to my wife's heart, and she willingly let me in.

I thought to myself, *I wish I could keep things this good between us forever.*

Of course, that is impossible, since every relationship hits a rough spot now and then, but I learned the most important relationship lesson of my life that day on my honeymoon:

We are mirrors to the people around us. The people we love are looking at us and asking the questions, "How am I doing? Am I talented? Am I valuable? What am I worth to you? Is there anything about me that makes you proud?" And whatever answer we give them, they believe!

The Gift of Love

Give your lover the gift of a special name. Make it unique between you and your lover. In addition to calling her sweetheart and honey, make up a name just for her.

As men, we have the ability to help produce the kind of wife we want simply by the words we say. If you shower your wife with compliments and encouragement she will be happier. If you tell her how valuable she is to you on a regular basis, she will have a growing sense of self-confidence and productivity. If you point out her strengths and abilities, she will be much more willing to use those strengths to meet your needs.

If on the other hand, you inundate her with insults and complaints, she will doubt her value to you. If you point out her shortcomings and run her down for being different from you, she will lose self-confidence. If you consistently criticize her and then ask her if she wants to get passionate, she will say, "Not with you!"

When I practice giving positive feedback, it is as if I have a mirror on my chest that my loved ones are looking at and making positive conclusions about who they are. When I resort to criticism and negative feedback, it's like having a broken mirror on my chest, with lots of cracks and distortions. I am defying the ones I love to feel good about themselves despite my evaluation. The message I send out is my choice, and it takes a lot of determination to choose to be positive. The fact is, no one is perfect. Your wife will do things that disappoint you. She will do things that inconvenience your life and interrupt your plans. She will spend money differently than you, treat friendships differently than you, and do tasks differenly than you. You will get discouraged with her, angry with her, disappointed with her, and irritated with her by the very things you love about her. It is your choice whether you will respond to the positive or the negative.

One of the mysteries of intimate relationships is that the things you love most about your spouse are the very things that irritate you most. Your wife's creativity may have attracted you to her, but her lack of organization at your house drives you crazy. Her dramatic personality may have enticed you because she brought so much energy and freshness to your life, but her overreactions now make you feel like life will never be under control. Or maybe her deliberate, organized approach to life made you feel like you had found someone who could help keep your life together, but her attention to details makes you feel like life has no spontaneity. Perhaps you thought the softness of her approach to life and attention to all your needs made you feel like your house would be a perpetual sanctuary, but now you feel smothered because she has no specific goals for her own life and you feel responsible for the direction of both your lives.

Appreciate the Great Performances

In my relationship with Pam, I was given a crash course in this principle early in our first year together. We were enjoying one of those cozy nights together talking through our life when I must have said the wrong thing. I don't even remember what I said, but I do remember thinking it could not have been bad enough to get the response I encountered.

A Little Extra

Inform your wife of her value to you by telling her friends what a great lady she is and let them tell her how you feel.

—⁓—

A friend and I were going on a retreat together. The friend phoned my house and my husband, Eric, answered. He told my friend that she would have a good weekend because, "Darlene is a lot of fun to be with."

Darlene Batrum, Bradley

Pam jumped up off the couch, shrieked the words, "You don't love me anymore!" ran into our bedroom, and threw herself on our bed, sobbing. It scared me to death! I had never seen anything like it before. I didn't know whether Pam was serious or just putting on a show for me. One of the things that had attracted me to Pam was her vivacious personality and high energy level. It was flattering when we were dating and all that energy was directed at encouraging me, but when this happened I was flabbergasted and wondering what I had done to deserve this outlandish display of emotion.

Well, I sheepishly went to the bedroom, wondering if she would ever let me into *our* room again. I sat down next to her on the bed and asked her what I had done. She murmured at me, "You mean you don't know?" Then she buried her head in the pillow again and resumed her convulsive sobbing. I sat there feeling like an idiot. I knew that Pam expected me to say something but what that something should be was way beyond my comprehension. So I just sat there and said nothing.

After a few minutes, Pam sat halfway up, looked at me with disgust, and asked, "Well, aren't you going to say anything?"

I wanted to say, "Hi, my name is Bill. Have you seen the woman I married anywhere around here?" Instead I said something really profound like, "Well, what do you want me to say?"

After realizing she had won this encounter, she decided to let me off the hook and forgive me for being a red-blooded neanderthal who had no clue into the emotional nuances of intimacy. I would like to say that I figured out how to handle

---

Let Her Know You Love Her

There is nothing a woman loves more than your undivided attention. Plan a day just for you and your wife and wait on her every need. Pay special attention to the little things you can do for her that she normally does for herself.

—∿∿—

I had been away on a business trip. When I flew in, my husband met me at the airport and whisked me away to a beach side inn. He spent the next day completely serving me—even to the point of taking off my shoes and socks, dumping out the sand, then putting them back on my feet and lacing them up. His words to me that week: "I finally have the best friend I've always wanted."

Faith Slusher, Lebec

The Gift of Love

Give your wife a gift to say, "Thank you" after she has helped you reach a significant goal, such as a college degree, promotion, buying a house, or losing weight. Match the gift to the goal—rings, bracelets, and other jewelry are always a hit.

—⁓—

When I completed my Master's degree in counseling, my husband gave me a bracelet that reads, "This is for all the major accomplishments thus far in your life. You are a great mom, you are a great wife, you are a great counselor.

Katie Turner, Bakersfield

these types of situations on my own, but the truth is that I was a miserable failure. She won every one of these encounters. I even think that she was encouraged to keep these outbursts up because she won them all so handily.

It took a visit from my brother-in-law to set the record straight. He was at the house when one of these dramatic performances happened. I said the wrong thing, Pam erupted into a melodramatic display, then ran to the bedroom and threw herself on the bed. I was embarrassed to have anyone else see this because I didn't have the faintest idea how to make this little problem of mine go away. I looked at Bret with a stupefied look on my face, revealing my obvious ineptness. I had a sense that this was a test to see if I would put Pam's needs before the needs of her brother. I could tell

Talking It Over

Questions for you:

When you spend romance money on your wife how do you feel? caring? attentive? intelligent? suave? rich?

When you've captured your wife's heart and she looks at you in her special, sexy way, which of the following statements gets closest to expressing what you feel?

"You have never looked better to me!"

or

"I am sure glad I was smart enough to marry you!"

Questions for her:

What is the most romantic thing I have done for you?

What romantic act do you wish I would do more often?

How do you feel when I bring you flowers?

Pam wanted to see if I would come to her rescue or if I would stay with Bret.

What happened next was astounding. Bret got up out of his seat and walked into our bedroom. Out of curiosity, I followed him to see what a little brother could possibly do to address this incredible display of emotional energy. He stopped about three feet from the bed and started clapping. Then, in his best announcer voice, he said, "And now presenting the Montgomery Award for best actress to Pam Farrel for her performance in *Tormenting Your Husband.*"

I thought for sure that Bret and I would never get out of this alive. How could he make fun of her at such an intense and poignant moment? How could he be so insensitive to the fragile needs of a newlywed bride? You can imagine my surprise when Pam stopped crying, looked up from her pillow, tried to glare at Bret, and then started laughing!

I had been had again. What looked to me like a genuine emotional crises was more of an extravagant way of making sure our love was strong enough to handle the storms of life.

From Pam's Heart

At a recent speaking engagement, I stepped up to the lectern, smiled at the audience, then looked down. There on the lectern was a hand mirror with a message written on it, "You are a beautiful woman of God." I was distracted. I had to work hard on focusing—but I didn't care because I was loved! That mirror hangs on the wall, reminding me daily that I am loved by a man who drove miles to deliever a surprise message to me.

Encouraging Words

Write out, on a small piece of paper, a compliment you will give your wife at a time when she is feeling unattractive. Put the paper in your wallet or organizer and practice it periodically until the opportunity presents itself.

—⚉—

Being seven months pregnant and feeling very uncomfortable and self-conscious, I didn't want my husband, Rob, to look at me after coming out of the shower. His response to me was, "Honey, young, old, fat, skinny, pregnant or not, you are absolutely beautiful to me!"

Michelle Anderson, Lathrop

Bret was able to see right through it and gave me a way of surviving Pam's emotional strength. I had a choice to make at this point. On the one hand, I was upset that I had been caught up in this emotional outburst. I was disappointed that life had to include this type of interaction between a man and a woman. I found myself tempted to wish that Pam was different. On the other hand, I was enticed by her emotional strength. If I was to engage in an outburst like the ones Pam was able to display, I would be exhausted. Yet she seemed to be energized by these displays and better prepared to face life when they were over. It took me awhile but I finally came to the conclusion that the vivacious, bouncy, emotionally vibrant personality of Pam that I loved so much was also the source of the melodramatic moments in our relationship. When I learned to be thankful for both sides of Pam's intense approach to life, I

Building Anticipation

Build anticipation in your wife's heart by putting a sign in a public place that says you love her and have missed her.

—⚶—

When I had to be away from my husband for five days he made an eighteen foot banner that he draped across a freeway overhang for me to see when I came home!

Becky Miller, Tehachapi

found it much easier to navigate through the uncomfortable situations and not take them so personally. I've even learned to give her a few standing ovations for great performances.

Use Your Imagination

Type the words to a song that describes your love for your wife. Print it on decorative paper and frame it. Give it to your lover with a note that says, "You have created a melody in my heart."

I wanted Pam to know that I would always be there for her, so I took six pictures and the words to one of the songs from our wedding and put them in picture frames. I then connected all these frames together in one display. I gave this to Pam as a present with a note telling her she could count on me in her life. It now hangs on the wall in our bedroom as a constant reminder of the gift of our love.

—*Bill Farrel*

The Gift of Love

Buy your wife a modeling experience. Look in the yellow pages and find a custom dress shop where your wife will be waited on. You can have a seat while someone else brings clothes to her. You can all *ooh* and *ahh* over her as she models.

———

Larry went to a dress shop and picked out what he thought was the perfect "Cinderella" dress. He arranged for me to have fittings and all the women in the shop were amazed at a man who would go to such great lengths so that his wife could feel like a princess.

Donna Joplin, Atascadero

3

The Sure Thing

Love is an irresistible desire to be
irresistibly desired.

—ROBERT FROST

oesn't it feel good when your wife thinks you're the greatest? We men give incredible power to our wives in being able to affect our attitude, our ego, and our decisions. Your wife may never fully understand the ability she has to change your state of mind and the influence she has on the outcome of your decisions.

How do you get your wife to think you are the man of her dreams rather than a nightmare she can't get away from? How do you keep her believing in you so that your efforts at romance are effective? There are a few things that are so fundamental to loving your wife that they warrant attention on a daily basis.

Be Positive: There is nothing more attractive in a man than a positive attitude. Life throws its share of challenges our way, and we are all tempted to get negative. But last time I checked, whining, complaining, and pity parties were not on the list of characteristics women are looking for in men.

✦ *How to Pick Up Your Wife:* Life with you is a never-ending journey of love and grace.

The Great Escape

Plan a getaway around your favorite sport. Buy tickets to the game, arrange easy transportation like a cab or bus, and rent a room so you can relax after the game. Draw your wife into the experience by taking her shopping before the game for a new outfit to help her brave the elements. Make sure you tell her during the game how good she looks and how proud you are to be seen with her.

It takes almost no energy to be negative—all you have to do is stop growing. Being positive, on the other hand, requires a deliberate decision on your part to stay on top of life rather than letting life get on top of you. It inspires confidence as you demonstrate in everyday commitments that you are a winner.

Your wife will especially appreciate your efforts at being a winner in life. Because women have a spaghetti approach to life, they have the tendency to get overwhelmed. They are constantly integrating the affairs of their life by getting in touch with them emotionally. Most of the time our wives are masters at juggling the details of life, because they are so in touch with it all. But sometimes Pam can feel an overwhelming number of emotions, and see so many situations needing to be addressed that it feels like a tidal wave breaking on the shore of her life. She needs a lifeguard to come alongside and remind her that the waves are not as big as they appear. From the middle of the surf they look a lot bigger than they do from the shore! If you have a positive attitude, you will act as the lifeguard in your wife's life, and you will help her surf life's challenges.

Be Confident: You have what it takes to love your wife! That is why she married you. But an interesting thing happens to almost all married couples: Over time, the characteristics you used to love became the areas that irritate you the most. And the aspects of your personality that captured your wife's heart are the same patterns that now frustrate her. The bad news is that your relationship will have its share of

---

From Pam's Heart

Recently, five minutes before I was to walk out the door to a speaking engagement, I made the awful discovery that one of our sons had accidently thrown away a brand new medical prescription worth $141—and of course the trash had been collected so the much needed medication was long gone. I called the pharmacy and the doctor trying to seek a quick solution, but with every call I got roadblocks. Bill walked in the door from work and I quickly explained the situation. Bill's reply, "Let me handle it. You have more important things to do right now." Then he kissed me, held me for a moment, and opened the door with a wink and a smile. At that moment, I felt valued. (I also felt like skipping the speaking engagement and whisking Bill to the bedroom to say "Thanks!" But alas, that had to wait until after the engagement!) Many times I love feeling self-sufficient and capable, but every once in awhile it is still terrific to have a knight in shining armor ride in to save the day.

A Little Extra

Hang in there when your wife is sick. She usually has to keep going, so take over the household chores and bring her food and medicine while you encourage her to rest.

—⚬⚬—

Years ago I suffered a nervous breakdown. My husband committed to caring for me at home while I saw a counselor on an outpatient basis. During this time, my husband cared for my physical, emotional, and spiritual needs. He bathed me and brushed my hair every day. He carried me to bed every night. He wrote me a personal daily devotion every morning. He fasted for me three times a week. He decorated our room the way he knew I would like because I was spending so much time there. Most importantly, I never sensed a loss of respect or adoration from him toward me during a time when I had nothing to offer.

Marci Williams, Oceanside

The Gift of Love

Buy a gift and store it in a secret place. When your wife has one of those exceptionally hard days, give her the gift as a reminder of your undying love.

—⚬⚬—

A week after having spent six days in the hospital with my youngest son for asthma, our basement flooded and a main sewer line broke. I decided I would clean it up, believing I would be more thorough than my husband. Afterward, while I was in an emotional cry, my husband got down on his knees in front of me and gave me a ring box. We were three weeks from our anniversary and he said I needed it now! It was the mother's ring I had been telling him I wanted for two years.

Megan Gibson, Lakewood

irritations. The good news is that every irritation is a window into a new discovery of love between you and your wife.

If you are going to keep the focus of your relationship on the attractive side of these characteristics, you need to be confident about your abilities and potential. Pam has been a fan of the fact that I am people-oriented. It makes her feel secure and valuable when we are together and my focus is on her. But, she has also been frustrated by the fact that I am people-oriented, and it can make her mad when I spend more time helping other people than she expected. Pam has to be flexible with her schedule to allow me to be myself. I have to be confident in the way I was created and not get

Talking It Over

Questions for you: When an unexpected crisis presents itself, do you feel threatened? invigorated? out of control? irritated? confused? heroic?

What helps you stay calm when circumstances turn hectic?

Questions for her: What activities help you grow in your personal life that I can actively support?

What have I done to help you grow that has been effective?

Building Anticipation

Put notes in unexpected places to remind her that she is in your heart even though you are not in the room.

—⁓—

My husband gets up at 2 A.M. everyday to commute to work. Before he leaves, he makes coffee and sets the timer so it is ready when I get up, and everyday he writes a note of encouragement and leaves it in my coffee cup!

Ginny McMillan, San Marcos

bent out of shape every time Pam struggles with my schedule. If not, the conversations about my personality will run over us.

My personality also has the potential to help other people find healthy ways of living, but it is a big responsibility to help others think through their lives. If I run away from the potential that I have been created with, Pam will struggle with the ability to trust me. If I don't trust myself, how can I expect Pam to trust in me?

Ask yourself these strategic questions:

What am I especially good at?

What have I been created to do?

Do I believe it is worthwhile and worth giving my heart to?

Your confident answers to these questions will inspire confidence in your wife and draw her to you.

Be Ambitious: Ambitious men bring security to the women in their lives. Your wife wants to know that life with you will be safe, secure, and satisfying. Part of this evaluation process involves financial potential. If you are ambitious and have well-defined goals, your wife will conclude that you have the potential to develop a financial plan that will provide for your family—even if you are not currently making enough money to cover the costs of life. If you are lazy or uninspired about the direction of your life, your wife will conclude that she has to carry you through life. As a result, she will not trust you with the needs of her heart and will nag you to be more productive.

The need to be ambitious does not just apply to the financial arena of life, though. If you are ambitious in your romantic goals, your wife will be filled with a sense of anticipation and hunger for your love. If your ideas for making your wife feel special are all small and you do not pull them off well, she will conclude you are "romantically challenged." If, however, some of your ideas are big and you don't get them all right, she will conclude you are an ambitious

Let Her Know You Love Her

Give your wife extra time to deal with a crisis in her life. Take the kids, provide transportation, cheer her on, and tell her to take the time that is necessary.

— w—

At 2 A.M. I received a call from Germany that my mom was dying of cancer. My husband said, "Don't worry about the four kids—Go!" I went and spent the last nineteen days of my mom's life with her.

Liz May, Paso Robles

Just the Two of Us

Set up your house like a luau. Buy some Hawaiian music and get your wife a lei. Borrow some plants from your friends and make your house look as much like a jungle as you can. Cook teriyaki chicken, rice, Hawaiian bread, and fresh fruit hors' douvres. Get a video that will teach the two of you how to do the Hula and take the lesson together. If you have been to Hawaii, get the photo album out and relive the experience.

lover who is not afraid to push to the edge to make her happy.

If you want to taste the fruit of love, you have to get out on the edge of the branches! Hugging the trunk of stability will be safe for you but there will be very little fruit. Out on the edge, where the wind blows and the branches creak, exciting things can happen. Sure, sometimes the branch breaks and you fall, but sometimes . . . !

Be Yourself: Your wife married *you*, not your imitation of someone else. Some of you are flamboyant, creative, and outgoing individuals. Some of you are steady, easy going, and introverted men. You will most effectively love your wife by being yourself and ignoring the stereotypes of what men are supposed to be.

Let's look at the difference between introverted and extroverted men. Extroverts tend to look at life from the outside in. That means they look at the situations around them and assess life according to how in control those things are. For instance, extroverts judge relationships based on the external characteristics of the friendship. They ask questions like, "Are we spending enough time together? Have we talked this through to its conclusion? Am I fulfilling my responsibility toward you?"

Extroverts assess their career based on how well it is going in terms of goals. They ask themselves, "Am I progressing in the pursuit of my goals? Am I meeting the expectations of those I must report to? Am I productive in my areas of responsibility?" Extroverts develop their spiritual life based on the activity of spiritual growth. They ask, "Am I spending enough time in Bible study? Is my prayer life active

---

Use Your Imagination

Turn your bedroom into heaven: Buy some dry ice. Put it in the sink in your master bathroom. Turn on the hot water just enough to fill the sink and slowly drain out the overflow. The dry ice will create a cloud approximately 2 feet deep in your room. Invite your wife in to dance with you in heaven.

—⁓—

My husband had disappeared into the bedroom and was gone for about thirty minutes. He told me he had a surprise and would come get me when he was ready. When he finally called me in, I opened the door and was met by clouds of mist on the floor billowing up around our bed. On the pillow was a note that read, You are my angel. Let's spend the night in heavenly romance.

Jane, Atascadero

┌───┐

Surprise!

Plan a surprise party for your wife's birthday. If this seems like a daunting task, ask her best friend to help you. Her friend will be impressed and tell your lover what a great guy you are.

└───┘

enough? Is my church attendance active enough to promote spiritual growth?"

The introvert, on the other hand, looks at life from the inside out. An introvert is more interested in how he is doing on the inside and how the people around him are doing internally. An introvert judges relationships based upon how connected people are. He will ask questions like, "Am I at peace with myself and with the important relationships of my life? Is my wife happy? Have my wife and I connected to the point that we understand each other? Are we content?"

In his career, the introvert is interested in finding work to do that is inwardly satisfying. He wants to feel that his work is an expression of who he is on the inside. He wonders, "Is this career a good fit for me? Does this job leave opportunity for my needs to be met? Do I enjoy going to work? Can I be myself in this position?"

In his spiritual life, the introvert is most concerned with the closeness of his relationship with God. "Am I connected to God? Are the spiritual activities I am involved in personally satisfying to me? Is my church attendance a true reflection of who I am?"

In a marriage, extroverts need to be extroverts and introverts need to be introverts. An outgoing, productivity-minded man is not going to enjoy sitting around having long conversations with his wife, but he will be great at planning and implementing evenings and getaways. An easy going, contented man will struggle with the flamboyant, enticing activities of romance, but he will have great potential for connecting at an intimate level in conversation.

There are two significant road blocks to making this happen in most relationships. The extrovert gets frustrated and the introvert gets withdrawn. The extrovert gets frustrated because life is not efficient enough or fun enough. He gets discouraged with his family because they are late, boring, lazy, or careless. The introvert feels his own needs and

From Pam's Heart

On my twenty first-birthday, Bill wanted to do something very special as a gift. He took me to breakfast, then we worked out together, then he took me to get a facial and get my make-up done. After that, lunch and shopping for a new outfit at a boutique where they wait on you like a princess, bringing hand-picked clothes for you to model! The whole day was one surprise after another. When we arrived back at our apartment, I was greeted by a house full of people for a surprise party! The best part of the gift wasn't the clothes, or the party, but the time Bill spent planning each detail so I would feel cared for. The secret to amazing romance is time and detail because each moment echos "I loved you enough to pay attention to your heart!"

The Gift of Love

Use flowers as a gift for a special occasion. A rose for each year of marriage, a lily for each child, a carnation for each career accomplishment will tell her you are paying attention.

——⁂——

When we celebrated our first anniversary, my husband gave me a red and a white rose. The white one was in anticipation of the year to come. We just celebrated our thirty-seventh anniversary and like all the past years, I received the number of roses for the year of our anniversary and one white rose. I'm glad the Lord has provided these years and also the money for him to buy thirty-seven roses plus one!"

the needs of those around him so deeply that he can get overwhelmed. He has a tendency to feel responsible for making those around him happy. If his skill level or maturity level is not sufficient to keep up with the needs around him, he will feel that he is going to fail and may shut down or become withdrawn to try to maintain peace.

As men, we need to embrace our uniqueness and grow in it. Those of us who are introverted need to develop our conversation and compassion skills so that we can run with our desire to be connected with our wives. Those of us who are extroverted need to focus on our planning and coordination skills so that we keep our wives looking ahead to the next great time we are going to spend together.

Encouraging Words

Select a day each month to deliberately compliment your lover. Make each compliment personal and handmade. Write a note, elaborate on a card, or draw a picture. Tell her this is a message straight from your heart. It might be awkward but she will love you for sharing yourself.

—⁂—

My husband of fourteen and a half years celebrates our anniversary every month. And he counts each month, such as 14.1, 14.2, 14.3,and so on. Sometimes the gift is a song he writes (usually silly in content) or a picture he draws in a card. Sometimes he brings a milkshake home from our favorite coffee shop. Every month he remembers a gift that comes from the heart.

Krista Fisher, Tehachapi

We have been married for fifty-two months now! I know this sounds funny, but on the first of every month my husband gives me a card. The card is full of loving thoughts of me and the joy of being married to me. We try to go out to dinner—or at least ice cream!

Wilma Fanders, Fallbrook

The Gift of Love

Give your wife a gift on a day when it is not expected. Make it a practical gift that affirms her strengths. A briefcase, business card case, or gift certificate for a new organizer will tell her you value her work. A needed kitchen appliance, new china, or permission to purchase new silverware will tell her you treasure her nurturing commitment.

—⁂—

Paul and I have been married eleven years. Every monthly anniversary of our wedding day, Paul gives me a gift! It is always something tangible and lasting so when I see it or use it, I will remember that he loves me. It's not the expense of the gift that warms my heart—it is the fact that he thinks of me and goes out of his way in his busy life to say, "I love you!"

Gail Wozniak, Newport Beach

Talking It Over

Questions for you: Do you consider yourself to be
                      introverted or extroverted? How
                      does this help your wife's life?
                      How does this complicate your
                      wife's life?

                      What is your favorite character-
                      istic about your wife? Write it
                      out in a note and explain how
                      this characteristic enhances your
                      life, then mail it to her.

Questions for her: What do you most like to do
                      with your free time?

                      What do you do that makes you
                      feel like you are being completely
                      yourself?

―∞―

The Great Escape

Rent a car you would never buy for yourself—a
Porsche, Corvette, or a convertible—and plan a tour
from one romantic inn to another. Your local travel
agent will have a list of inns close to you or you can get
a guide book at your local bookstore. You can brag about
the performance of your auto while she brags about the
environment of the inn.

4

Building Anticipation

Grow old with me! The best is yet to be.
—ROBERT BROWNING

I was having one of those days! I was working hard, and there seemed to be no break on the horizon. I knew I was going to be wrapped up with work all day, and the next two were already heavily scheduled. I love my work, but what I really wanted was to be home with Pam. I was distracted by intimate thoughts about her, and I was having a hard time concentrating on the task at hand. It occurred to me that I had to run by the house to pick up some work papers I had left on the kitchen counter, but I had only a few minutes to be home because I was up against a deadline.

I wanted Pam to know that I was distracted, but I couldn't get carried away. So I thought about what I could say to let her in on the desire of my heart as I drove toward the house. As I walked in the door to get the papers, I took time to look for her. I found her in the office, wrapped my arms around her waist, looked her confidently in the eyes, and said, "I wish I

❦ *How to Pick Up Your Wife:* If I say, "You have a beautiful body," will you hold it against me?

Encouraging Words

Tell your wife that she is the woman of your dreams. Let her know she is in your fantasies. Describe one of your fantasies and how she is the center of it.

—⁓—

My husband says his fantasies during intimacy are about our earlier times together—even after 45 years of marriage!

---

was independently wealthy and could stay home and love you all day long."

I then kissed her, picked up my papers, and headed back to work. The next couple of days were just as busy as I thought they would be. I had to leave early in the morning, and I didn't get home until I was exhausted from fourteen hours of work each day. But the third day was a different story!

I had the day off, and we had planned to get some chores done around the house. We got the kids off to school, and I started making plans to attack my chores. Pam kept following me around, acting very interested. She was saying flirty things and giggling at everything I said. She was making up reasons to touch me. She was flaunting herself in front of my list so that I was unable to focus on our plan for the day.

I had assumed that sex was out of the question this morning because I had been virtually gone for three days. I know that Pam needs lots of quality time together to be in the mood, and lately we'd had anything but quality time. I was enjoying this attention, and was secretly wishing this could happen every day, but I was puzzled by the sudden rush of enthusiasm on Pam's part.

Eventually I stopped trying to be task oriented and asked her, "What's up with all this attention? Don't get me wrong, I love it! But I don't understand why you are so excited when we haven't spent time together."

She looked me in the eyes with my favorite sensuous gaze and said, "You wish you were independently wealthy and could love me all day long."

The anticipation that had been building in her heart for the last three days led to one of the best memories I have of the potential of intimate love. I learned that day that building anticipation is one of the most powerful aspects of romance—and one of the most attractive activities of foreplay!

From Pam's Heart

My favorite words to hear Bill whisper have got to be, "I want to be lost in your love" or "Pam, I love getting lost in you." Those words have been sent via the voicemail, whispered in public settings for my ears only, said as Bill and I have danced under the moonlight of our patio or after the kids have been sent to bed—and many times in moments much more passionate. Everytime Bill whispers, those words, a fever washes through my soul, and my heart, mind, and body long to be given to him. I feel my love has power, that it is the shelter to his soul, and I want to give it often and with abandon when I hear those words . . . "lost in your love."

Memories

Build a memory between you and your wife by choosing a phrase that you write on a note on a regular basis. This phrase will become a memory for her of the security of your love for her.

—ⱳ—

My husband says, "Have I told you I love you today?" He leaves I love you today notes all over the house—once on the edge of a new roll of toilet paper!

Darleen Bewley, Madera

So, how do you build anticipation in your wife? Here are some ideas to experiment with to help your wife look forward to your intimate times together:

Send her notes: Your wife loves words. A short note from you is a treasure in her heart. A long note from you lingers in her heart like a beautiful sunset that adds color to the whole sky. She loves to hear from you often and personally.

Send her cards: Often guys are at a loss for what to say to their wives. We have thoughts in our head and desires in our heart, but we don't have the faintest idea how to put them into words that will touch her heart. Greeting cards are a great way to say what you want to say without coming up with the profound thoughts all on your own. I recently sent Pam a card that said on the front:

I Love You!
I Want You!

I Need You!
You Mean Everything to Me!

The Message inside read,

"That's All I Wanted to Say."

Pam still has that card taped to her mirror in our bathroom to remind her about my desire to be with her.

Non-sexual affection: Women love to be touched. Women need to be touched. But when all touching is perceived as sexual overtures, your wife will begin to feel pressure every time you are affectionate with her. As a result, she will avoid you to free herself from the demands she thinks you are putting on her. For your wife, romance and sex are related to every aspect of her life. It is a seamless experience for her. The way you hold hands with her in public will determine the way she responds to you in the bedroom. Make it a goal to touch your wife every day in a way that says, *I love you as a person, I love you as a lover, and I love you as a friend.*

Plan your spontaneous encounters: Your wife will be much more spontaneous with you if you have communicated with her a plan for staying in love. When she can

The Gift of Love

Give your spouse the hug of her life. Wrap your arms around your wife and whisper in her ear, "I love you and I am happy to be stuck with you." Then hold her firmly, yet tenderly, as you slowly count to 100. When you are done, whisper in her ear again, "I love you in more ways than I can count."

Just the Two of Us

Design a date around your favorite movie. For instance, you might buy a card and write in it, "*I believe in you and me.*" Plan an afternoon of ice skating. Buy the soundtrack and rent the movie *The Preacher's Wife*. Spend the evening watching the movie and dancing with one another.

———

My husband did a whole date based on the word, "Always." He engraved a plaque that said, How long will I love you? Always. It also included the dictionary's definition of always. He played the song, Always. We watched the movie, Always. And he bought a balloon and card that said—you guessed it—Always!

Jennie Abernathy, Suisun City

look at the calendar and know that romance is a priority, her desire rises up inside her. My friend, Jim Conway, says that women are like electric ovens when it comes to romance and sex. You turn on the electric burner and it appears nothing is happening. You can put your hand on the burner and it feels like cold steel. But if you keep it on it will become red hot. It can become so intense that you panic and turn it off. But it doesn't turn off! It stays hot for a long time. This is difficult for men to relate to because we operate like gas stoves—instant on, instant off. If you want your wife to be consistently responsive to you, give her experiences to which she can look forward. Plan dates and getaways for her to anticipate.

Call her on the phone: Words are like dessert to your wife. She loves to talk and she loves to hear your voice. When her day is interrupted by your voice, she begins to look forward to being with you.

Talking It Over

Questions for you: How would you feel if your wife planned a secret getaway for just the two of you?

When you get away with your wife and you both are relaxed, which of these words best describe how your wife looks to you: beautiful? sexy? cute? sultry? amorous? athletic? regal? Why did you choose that particular word?

Question for her: If we had two weeks off and could afford to go anywhere in the world on vacation, where would you like to go?

What do you think is the most romantic spot on earth?

Of the places we have been, what is the most romantic?

The Gift of Love

Give your wife a gift on each of your children's birthdays.

—⚏—

When our children celebrated birthdays, Kent would always give me a box of my favorite chocolates with a card saying the child could not have a birthday without me!

Alline Lihme, Julian

If you have a date coming up, call her and say, "I am really looking forward to spending this Friday night with you. I just called to tell you I can't wait."

If you are going on vacation in the near future, call her answering machine and tell her how distracted you are at work thinking about spending an entire week getting reacquainted with her.

If your fifteenth anniversary is coming up, call her every day for fifteen days before your anniversary and let her know all the reasons why you are looking forward to celebrating your love on the date of your anniversary.

Read poetry or share a song with her: Because women love words so much, poems and songs have special meaning for them. The manipulation of words so they reach the heart is a special gift for our wives that warms their hearts. This is especially helpful for men who have a hard time figuring out what to say. If you feel clumsy with words, get a poetry book and start accumulating the words of songs to share with her at strategic times.

You may want to try your hand at writing your own poems for your lover. The quality of the poem is not nearly as important as the time you spend lovingly putting your thoughts into words. I have seen Pam respond just as favorably to very simple poems as she has to long and involved ones. The first time I saw Pam's heart melt because of my poetry was the day I proposed to her. I wrote her the following poem just prior to asking her to marry me:

Stay with Me

Stay with me, stay with me.
Come and live your life with me.
Together we can rearrange our plans.

We can dream our dreams and we can make our plans.
And we can make them work, just you and I.
If you will . . .

Stay with me, stay with me.
Come and seek our Lord with me.
Together we'll become two into one.

We'll pray by our choice and we'll listen for His voice.

He'll lead us to the greatest life there is.
I want you to . . .

Stay with me, stay with me.
Come and give your love to me.

You are to me what no one else could be.

You light up my life and you treat me like a king.
Apart from you, I don't want a thing
but to . . .

Stay with you, stay with you.
I want to give my love to you
And be to you what no one else could be.

I'll treat you like my queen.
You're the most beautiful girl I've seen.
I love you now and I always will.
So won't you . . .

Stay with me, stay with me.
Come and live your life with me.
Together we'll become two into one.

Surprise!

Plan a surprise getaway for your lover in cooperation with family members or good friends. Have them visit at your house. As they leave, have them take the kids as you whisk her away for a weekend of relaxation.

—⁓—

We had friends from out of town with us from Thursday until late Friday. My husband arranged for his parents to care for our two small children. All I knew was that we were going to drop off the kids, then take our friends out to dinner before taking them to the airport. After we sent them off, my husband drove right past the freeway exit that leads to our home. He just kept driving. All my stuff had been packed in the trunk of the car. He had packed for me! I had to buy a few things—so what! I remembered I had mentioned to my husband that I wanted an adventure. How romantic! We had a wonderful weekend falling in love again.

Sue Guinn, Saugus

The amazing thing about words is that it doesn't take very many to leave a lasting impression. Pam and I bought a package of Magnetic Poetry a couple years ago. These are words, letters, and punctuation marks that allow us to leave romantic messages on the refrigerator for each other. Two simple verses that captured Pam's imagination are:

You, me, tonight?

I am a prisoner in a dream of you.

Send Invitations: Instead of asking her out on dates in a nonchalant manner, try sending her an invitation in the mail with an RSVP on the bottom. She will feel like you spent hours planning this time together and will be very impressed. You can make up your own invitations using a computer program, or you can purchase one at a store and fill it out. To add even more splendor to your invitation, you might try putting some of your aftershave on it, sending it with flowers, or attaching it to a helium filled balloon.

Send a thank you: After a very special night together, send her a thank you note for the memory. After a great

Use Your Imagination

Spend a night together at the same place you spent your wedding night. Try to remember as many details as possible and recreate them for her.

—⁓—

My husband was always doing things to surprise me. My favorite was for our twenty-fifth wedding anniversary. Without my knowledge, he made reservations at the Fairmount Hotel in the very same room we had on our wedding night.

When I saw my husband packing, I asked him where he was going. He said, "San Francisco, want to come?"

I said, "I can't. I'd have to give my boss notice."

He told me, "I've done that! I have two plane tickets."

We had an even greater time on our anniversary than we did on our honeymoon!

Norma Wells, Long Beach

date, send a note thanking her for being a great friend. When she is willing to try something new or adventurous in your sexual encounters, leave her a note ranting about what a great lover she is becoming. You will probably find that she saves these notes and reviews them periodically. Her confidence will grow as she feels appreciated by you. Her desire to please you will be rewarding for her because she is convinced that you are paying attention. A thank you for the *last* great time with her will build anticipation for the *next* great time.

Building Aniticipation

Lead your wife on a treasure hunt. Put a note on the front door inviting her on the adventure. Guide her from one note to another until she reaches her destination, where you will be romantically awaiting her arrival.

—✼—

I came home from work to a note on the front door, which led to another note, then another, finally ending up in the bedroom. The room was lit with candles, and music was playing. The final note said to get ready for my husband, and to turn on the light on the master bedroom patio. He entered the room for a romantic evening together.

Lorraine Solomon, Canyon City

5

Is the Fairer Sex Really Fair?

I have seen only you,
I have admired only you,
I desire only you.

—Napolean Bonaparte

*P*am was bouncing around the house with a curious smile on her face. I was intrigued by the flirtatious way she was acting, and I was starting to think this was going to be a good night. For about an hour the atmosphere in our home was as comfortable as I have ever seen it. Life was good and love was easy. Then the air suddenly grew cold. Pam's attitude toward me was icy and the freedom was gone. I didn't understand what had happened. She changed so quickly from an amorous, fun-loving girlfriend to a sullen, distant, hard-to-understand woman. I didn't comprehend what I had done that was so bad that I should get shut out of the fun.

I, in turn, saw a transformation in myself. I went from being so interested in Pam that I followed her around like

---

✦ *How to Pick Up Your Wife:* You may not be perfect, but you are perfect for me.

A Little Extra

Decide now that you will let your wife know she is more important than a possession of yours that becomes lost or broken. When the inevitable happens say to her, "That might have been expensive, but you are the only priceless thing in my life."

⁓

I lost my ring. My husband helped me look for it for six hours. We looked everywhere but couldn't find it. The center stone of the ring was from his mother's wedding ring. I was devastated! He went to bed. I sat in the living room and cried. He finally noticed I was missing and came to look for me; he sat down beside me, took my hands in his, and said, "Amy, I just want you to know that whatever happens, things are just things. I love you." All of a sudden something told me to look under the sofa—again. There was the ring!

Amy Lewandoski, Oak View

Indiana Jones searching for valuable treasures, to a depressed, angry man who was feeling cheated out of a satisfying night of passion. And all I had done was comment on her schedule!

"Pam, I would really like us to spend time together tomorrow."

"Hey, Bill, that sounds good. Thanks for thinking about me."

"I'll be home around six. Could you have dinner ready?" I asked Pam with the idea that we would have a lot more time together if we could have dinner with the kids and get them to bed. Her eruption took me by surprise.

"That's all you love me for, isn't it? You have never thought my stuff was as important as yours," Pam shot at me with body language that could have stopped traffic on the freeway.

"Pam, I didn't mean that. I just thought we would . . ."

"You are always thinking about you! When is it my turn to be taken care of? I don't think you will ever understand!"

With that, she headed upstairs and my hope for the evening was put to bed. I walked around the house fuming, sure that God had made a mistake when he created woman. I was convinced that there was no way to figure this out. I have since discovered that every man's wife tests her husband to answer one very important question: "Am I more valuable to you than anything else in your life?"

Security is your wife's most pervasive need. She longs to know that life with you is *safe*. She wants to be assured of physical safety, financial safety, social safety, and emotional safety. She doesn't mean to be unreasonable about this, but it is a constant need for her to know she is secure with you. To build confidence that she is safe, she will throw tests your way to confirm that her security is intact. To put it into perspective, your wife needs to have her security met as often as you would like to have sex with her.

The strategy for passing these tests is simple in concept and complicated in practice. The goal is as follows: *Address the security need, and the issue at hand becomes manageable.* If you keep this in mind, you will find that most issues can be discussed with your wife in a sane and logical fashion. If, however, you do not get this one right, you will be left with an intricate web of conversation to try to untangle. The issue will become so layered and will change so many times that you will get lost in the discussion. Your interaction with your wife will be completely void of the kind of logic you understand. You

Surprise!

Hide a surprise gift among the daily routine of her life. Put a ring on the chord of the iron. Place a card on top of the stack of plates. Nestle a bubble bath packet in with her lingerie. Hang a new nightgown on the hanger under her coat. Be creative and brighten up her everyday life.

—⁓—

Day after day when I was pregnant, I lowered myself into my recliner as only a pregnant woman can. One night, during my ninth month, we had company come visit. In the middle of conversation, my husband asked me, "Honey, can you get me a glass of water?" I had just lowered myself into the recliner! He was sitting comfortably in a chair, but because we had guests, I got up thinking, I'll talk to him later! There in the cabinet, next to the glasses, was a pair of sapphire earrings that I had admired earlier!

Mary Carillo, Whittier

will conclude that your wife is illogical, irrational, and unreasonable as she beats you to a pulp with her overpowering skills of conversation.

Test #1: The "What if I Waste Money" Test

"Do you like it?" Jennifer asked with a coy look in her eye.

Steven was speechless as he stared at the $150 watch that Jennifer had just given him for his thirtieth birthday. Steven had pointed out the watch to Jennifer in the wish list catalog and she had acted quickly—much more quickly than he had hoped. The budget for birthday presents this year was $50.

He had a dilemma. He had to come up with a strategic response to her generosity. She had irresponsibly spent more money than they agreed, and she was looking very proud of herself. If he said he didn't like it, she would be crushed. If he didn't disagree with her decision, he was afraid she would think it was okay to spend more money than they budgeted. He could see only disaster. On the one hand, he was going to encourage poverty. On the other hand, he was going to encourage chastity.

This test is a way for your wife to uncover whether she is more important than your money. If she perceives that she is more important than the budget you have agreed to, she will be very reasonable and easy to talk with. If she concludes that money is more valuable to you than she is, she will test your money management skills to the limit.

Use Your Imagination

Pray with your wife often. There is nothing more intimate than the act of prayer. When you pray, your wife gets a good look into the depths of your heart—and it softens her heart toward you.

—⚏—

Every night and every morning my husband prays for me.

Linda Huek, Carlsbad

Just the Two of Us

Free or nearly free dating ideas:

1. Take a walk on the beach.

2. Take a walk in your neighborhood.

3. Take a walk in the mall.

4. Go to a park near your house and swing next to each other while you talk about the dreams and goals of your life.

5. Pop popcorn, set up two comfortable chairs in your house facing your television, rent a romantic movie, and have a home night at the movies.

6. Choose a special place for the two of you to watch the sunset. Take cheese and crackers and something to drink. Lay a blanket out on the ground and describe the sunset to one another as you share how it makes you feel about each other.

7. Buy a book of stories or poems. Go to a coffee house or ice cream parlor and take turns reading to one another.

8. Take your wife to a park or the gym, and teach her how to play basketball (or your favorite sport). Then let her teach you how to be a cheerleader (or her favorite sport).

9. Go to a music store. Spend time choosing songs from demos that remind you of each other. Each time you find one, have your lover put on the headphones and listen to your words of love.

10. Put a bowl of peanuts and a basket of pretzels on the kitchen counter. Put bottles of root beer, or your favorite drink, on ice. Clear your dining room and rent a video teaching you how to line dance. Get dressed up in western clothing and escort your wife to the dance floor for private lessons.

Test #2: The "Are You Willing to Waste Money?" Test

"Thanks for the flowers, honey. They are beautiful and they smell so good!"

Aren't you amazed at how flowers will change your wife's attitude? I, for one, have never thought that flowers would be a good present to receive. A cordless drill, a new fishing pole, or, a computer game maybe, but flowers? They are not practical. They do not last. They don't serve any useful purpose. But our wives love them. Why?

I have concluded that women love flowers because they are a waste of money. It is not that our wives want us to throw money away. They just need to know that we value them more than our money. When you spend money on presents for your wife that are temporary, she gets the message that she is supremely valuable to you. She concludes that she is vital to you, while your money is just a tool to help meet needs. When you fight her for the financial management of

The Gift of Love

Draw a picture of the gift you would like to give your wife. The personal touch of your art work will be the gift she treasures most.

―∽―

Once when we were really low on money, my husband drew a picture of a rose on a piece of paper and gave it to me. I keep that favorite flower in my Bible.

Mikki Anderson, Madera

Building Anticipation

Divide a gift you want to give your wife into a number of smaller gifts. Give the smaller gifts to her on consecutive days. Don't tell her how many days she will receive gifts until she gets the last one.

On Mother's day, ten days before my birthday, my husband gave me a strip of paper with the heading: Top 100 Things I Want to Thank You for (in no particular order). The sheet had only ten items on it, however. I thought he had just made a mistake on the heading and was grateful for the encouragement of ten traits he appreciated. To my surprise, each day from then until my birthday, he left a list of ten things somewhere in the house. Items ranged from teaching our kids Bible verses to cleaning up behind the cat and dog. On my birthday he left the final ten, which were paragraphs about the characteristics he valued in my life and character. I can't begin to describe how this touched me!

Lynn White, Vista

your life and never do anything frivolous for her, she gets the message that money is closer to your heart than she is.

When you periodically spend money on her without regard to your budget, it buys you space. She will more than make up for the cost by saving in other areas of your life. Her security will help make your finances secure.

Test #3: The "Are You Sincere?" Test

Your wife drops hints for weeks. She isn't feeling appreciated. She is starting to say crazy things like, "All you want me for is my body. You never romance me. You don't treat me special anymore. All I want is a meaningful relationship with you." In the midst of these, she talks about dates out on the town, flowers, cards, and candy.

You clue into her words and you plan the night. You arrange child care, select her favorite restaurant, and pick her up with flowers and chocolate in hand. You have had a long week and you're tired. You aren't really up for this evening, but you know she wants you to be more interested and more romantic. You are committed to doing the right things for her.

At first she seems flattered by your attempt to make her feel special, but over dinner the evening starts to get tense. She looks you in the eyes and says, "You only did this because you had to. You don't really want to do this, do you?"

You try frantically to rescue the evening with something like, "What do you expect from me? I did everything I

From Pam's Heart

I arrived at the hotel, unpacked my bag, and found a gift inside. The next morning I found another in my speaking notes, and every day for the next ten. Sometime during each day I would find a gift tucked somewhere unexpected. For the twelfth day of Christmas, I gave my true love a gift that he'll be sure to remember!

Encouraging Words

Tell your wife how smart you are to have chosen her to be your life partner. Let her know you could not have done better!

—⁓—

If I say negative things about myself, he says—"Be careful what you say—that's the woman I love that you're talking about."

Carolyn Calhoun, Fresno

thought you'd like. You are always telling me how you like dinner away from home so you can have a break from the chores and the kids. You are always dropping hints about flowers and cards. I did all this for you to show you I care about you."

"Well," she says with a little desperation in her voice, "it just doesn't seem like you really mean it. I don't think you did these things because you love me. I think you were nice to me tonight because you were afraid I would be hard to live with if you didn't."

The problem is, she is right. You *are* afraid she will be hard to live with if you don't treat her special. And now that you have done the things you think will work—things that have worked in the past—you are stumped by their failure. You think for sure that she will notice your desire to make her happy and that your relationship will become simpler. Then she drops the sincerity bomb. Not only do you have to do the right things, but you must mean them from the heart!

This test confirms your wife's security by reassuring her that she has first place in your heart. If she thinks that you just want to make peace, she will conclude that peace in your marriage is more important than her. If she thinks that your personal level of comfort and convenience is more valuable than she is, she will interrupt your comfort with her needs and demand that she own your heart.

Test #4: The "Fishing for Compliments" Test

"Do you notice anything different about me, honey?"

Doesn't this question send chills up and down your spine. By her statement, you know your wife has done something to

---

Talking It Over

Questions for you:
> How does it affect you when you succeed in meeting the security needs of your wife and she you are wonderful?
>
> Describe how you feel when your wife is feeling secure. Do you feel triumphant? successful? insightful?

Questions for her:
> What is the happiest experience of your life?
>
> What brings tears to your eyes?
>
> Why do you like movies that move you to tears?

The Gift of Love

Give your wife a massage. Your wife longs to be touched by you when it is centered on her well-being.

—⁓—

When I was pregnant, my husband bought a video tape on massage and started to give me a back rub each evening.

Cindy Pessotto, Escondido

change her physical appearance. If you guess correctly, you are a hero and intimacy will be close at hand. If you don't notice, you will be labeled insensitive and unobservant. If you guess wrong, you will be accused of just guessing to save your skin.

The preparation for this test is more important than recognizing the test. If you shower your wife with compliments consistently, you will develop grace for the times you miss the mark. Your wife will tend to overlook the awkwardness of your lack of attention to details when you fill her life with compliments.

Pam was sure she was going to impress me. She had been talking about a haircut for a few weeks. She asked my opinion of our mutual friends' haircuts and showed me pictures of women in magazines, asking me to evaluate how various hairstyles would look on her. I must admit that I did not find the exercise all that enjoyable—I don't regularly notice hairstyles unless they are outlandish or outright hideous.

Pam decided a haircut and permanent wave would be the strategic choice. She was sure I would love it and would swoon over her when she came home. She made the appointment, but didn't tell me she was going to see her beautician. I was supposed to notice and tell her how beautiful she was.

I noticed that night that something was different, but couldn't put my finger on it. So I didn't say anything—for five days! Pam never rescued me from my blindness. I could tell something was wrong but couldn't figure out what it was. Pam was cautious and very responsible, but not responsive. On the fifth day, I finally noticed her haircut and thought I would impress her with my powers of observation.

"Pam, your hair looks great!" I said triumphantly.

"Oh, you finally noticed. I thought maybe you had slipped into a coma. It's good to have you back."

Pam was more right than I like to admit. I was in a compliment coma, so wrapped up in my own world that I had stopped noticing what a beautiful wife I have. Fortunately, Pam gave me grace and didn't shut me out. She allowed

Encouraging Words

Write down the five abilities you admire most about your wife. Look for opportunities to tell her how much her friends would benefit if they had these same qualities.

—⚇—

Once when my husband and I were discussing a mutual friend he said, "What she needs is for you to give her lessons in self-confidence." I never knew my husband had that image of me until then.

Kristin Bennet, Visalia

A Little Extra

Go through your house and make a list of 30 valuable things. Every day for a month, tell your wife that she is more valuable than something on the list.

herself to be glad that I noticed even though it took me entirely too long.

Test #5: The "Am I More Important than Your Sleep?" Test

It was the last day of my honeymoon, and I had been enjoying what I believed to be the best of all possible worlds. I was in Lake Tahoe with the woman I loved, and I had been introduced to the guilt-free thrills of physical intimacy with my wife. The only down side was that we were out of money. But we were traveling the next morning to Pam's relatives to celebrate Christmas, and we knew there was money waiting for us there. We needed to get up very early to drive to Reno in order to catch our flight to Idaho, so I figured we should go to bed early enough to get a good night's sleep. This seemed very reasonable to me, but I forgot to ask my wife if that was what she had in mind.

The anticipation of this being the last night of our honeymoon led to a great time of sexual intimacy. What happened next was the beginning of new education for me. I have since learned that good sex winds women up—and they stayed wound up for a long time. During the next three hours, I heard about every boyfriend she had ever had in her life. The first was when Pam was eight years old and, as far as I could tell, there was not a year in her life when she didn't have a

From Pam's Heart

When our youngest son was two, I drove the car into the garage and parked it. I pulled the key out of the ignition, and Caleb pointed to the picture on the ring, "Daddy!" I smiled, "Yes! Daddy and Caleb," I responded, and I handed him the photo key chain. I walked around the car to take him out of his carseat, and, while I was walking around the car, he squeezed out of the carseat and stuck a key into the ignition—the right key! The car lurched forward as I frantically tried to get the door open. It was too late. The car crushed our brand new full-size freezer. A few more inches and the freezer would have gone through the living room wall! I grabbed the keys and Caleb, saw that he was all right, then carried him into the house, sobbing. I picked up the phone to call Bill. His secretary put me right through. "Bill . . ."

"Honey, what is it? What's wrong?" Through sobs and "I'm sorries" the story tumbled out. "Honey, you're okay, Caleb is okay. That's all that matters. You are much more important than a freezer to me. How can I help?"

Forgiveness and grace is the face of God's love. When Bill extends forgiveness, I am drawn to him. When he does something that irritates me, I remember the words of grace he's given me and I extend the same to him.

Talking It Over

Set some time aside periodically to ask your wife to help you understand her need for security. It is not a need that you feel, so she needs to fill in the gaps in your thinking. Ask questions like:

When you are walking alone to your car at night, what is it like for you?

What does it do for you when I am listening intently to you? When I am not listening?

When I succeed at passing one of the tests in this chapter, how does it affect you?

What does this statement mean to you: "She needs to know that life with you is safe?"

What makes you feel safe?

special relationship. She told me she wanted to share every detail of her life with me. She wanted me to know everything. As a young, idealistic husband, I concurred and thought it would actually be possible to listen to Pam with the same detail with which she was sharing herself.

I was holding my own for the first hour. I was getting restless during the second hour. The third hour was a disaster. In the middle of a sentence, I started to doze off, but caught myself in time to shift my body and find the alertness to continue listening without her realizing I was losing it. Some time after that it finally happened. I fell fast asleep while she was baring her soul. I awakened to a heart quake that registered 3.5 on our bed.

Pam was convulsively sobbing, murmuring, "I thought you loved me. How could you fall asleep on me? Am I really that boring?"

I thought these were honest questions! I thought Pam really wanted an answer to what she asked so I sat up in bed, looked her in the eyes, and said, "I really do love you. I am so sorry for falling asleep. Go ahead and finish. I will listen to you talk about the men who came before me but couldn't capture your heart."

Pam pushed the issue, "You don't really want to hear it. You are just saying you will listen because you have to."

Let Her Know You Love Her

Get actively involved with a difficulty you are having with one of your children. Ask, "What can I do to help?" when is it critical that I am here to assist with our child. Your attention to your child will lower your lover's stress level and make her more interested in you.

—⁓—

My husband had a job that entailed a four-hour commute each day. One of our children was in teenage rebellion, and we never knew what each day would bring. My husband came home each night instead of staying in the company apartment so I wouldn't have to hang in there alone. Praise God, that child responded and turned around!

Kit Davis, Vista

The Great Escape

If you have an especially prosperous year, plan a flight date. Call your travel agent and ask for ideas on going to a romantic city. Rent a car, stay in a nice hotel, eat dinner at a restaurant that is on top of one of the downtown buildings, and see a play or concert while you are there.

—⁓—

My spouse set up a secret date to San Francisco to see Phantom of the Opera. He arranged child care, and bought me a new dress, shoes, and a purse. It was a full day—lunch, the performance, and dinner. He said his gift to me that day was his 100 percent attention. I felt like a princess all that day and longer!

Joanne Carmazzi, Sacramento

With a little bit of desperation in my voice, I reassured her, "No, Pam, I really want to know. Every detail of your life is important to me."

"Do you really mean it?"

"Yes, Pam. I really mean it!"

"Okay," she said with a glint in her eye, "Then I want to tell you about the country western songs I listened to growing up." Then she started singing!

I had been out done again. Here I was trying to address Pam's stated concern, and, I was totally missing the real issue. The issue that was truly on Pam's heart was, "Bill, am I more important to you than your sleep? Are you willing to be tired to show me that I have first place in your heart?"

Test #6: The "Do You Notice Other Women" Test

This is one of the hardest to recognize and respond to strategically. Your wife asks you, "What do you think of that woman's haircut?"

At times the right answer is, "What woman?" as if you don't know that any other woman exists. During these times your wife will be touched by your dedicated affection and feel closer to you for protecting her unique value in your life. Other times, she will criticize you for being blind to her cosmetic priorities and will give you the cold shoulder.

At other times the right answer is, "Yes, I did. I think her haircut is cute. I even think you might look good in a style like that." One time she will be impressed that you would think about what would look good on her. The next time she will be offended you even noticed that other women had hair.

This test applies to noticing body types, clothing styles, modesty, and attitudes. We are required to be aware of the ploys and practices of women without really noticing that there are other women in the world. We need to treat all women with respect, but only our wives with interest. You are supposed to notice that your wife is the most beautiful of all women without ever comparing her to another woman.

Passing the Tests

The key to passing these tests is to consistently address the security need of your wife. If she is feeling secure in her relationship with you, she will extend grace to you in the areas where you fall short. If she perceives that she is the most important individual in your life, she will be much more relaxed about your deficiencies. So how do you address the security needs of your wife?

Listen for the tests. The reason we fail these tests so often is because our ears are dull to them. Your wife throws one of these tests your way and you don't recognize it. Because of this you try to apply your trusty male logic to the conversation and your wife gets frustrated with you. You don't understand that the big need for her is security, so you try to apply some more male logic to her emotional reversal. This only serves to finalize your defeat as she concludes that you don't understand. It is not that you don't want to help her, it is just that you are not used to identifying the tests.

Accept her need for security. No matter how much you may wish she was easier to love, the fact is she is a woman, and women have a need to feel secure. They are motivated by it, saddened by it, fulfilled by it, and frustrated by it. It is this need for security that caused her to find you so attractive. It is easy to accept this need when it causes her to curl up in your arms and want to meet all your needs, but it is another thing when this need cries out for attention. To find harmony in your relationship, you will have to find a way to say that it is okay that she needs security. Enjoy it when it's good and invest in it when it's hard. Don't ever try to figure it out, just master it.

Ask her to teach you. No man alive truly understands this mysterious aspect of women's lives. The best we can do is to learn. About the time you have figured it out, the need takes on a new look. There is only one of you in the relationship who understands this need for security, and you are not the one! Ask her to teach you about security.

6

Pulling Your Foot Out of Your Mouth

Because genuine love involves an extension of oneself, vast amounts of energy are required.

—M. SCOTT PECK, M.D.

O ne of the most frustrating parts of being a man is the tendency I have to put my foot in my mouth. I have made a hobby out of saying things in public that are quite embarrassing. I was once working a mother/daughter banquet where the daughters were modeling their mom's wedding dresses. To facilitate the schedule, we decided that we would serve the young ladies first, so they could eat the meal and then get dressed for the fashion show. I was playing the part of a sophisticated waiter serving dinner to these ladies when a middle-aged woman stopped me at one of the tables.

She said to me, "If I was a model would you serve me first?"

That's when I showed my true male colors. I looked at her with a big smile on my face and said, "Sure, but you would have a hard time convincing me that you are a model."

❦ *How to Pick Up Your Wife:* I have been around enough to know that I want to keep coming back to you.

Let Her Know You Love Her

Go out of your way to make up for a mistake your wife has made, but do not criticize her. Just say, "I love you," as you ride in on your white horse and save the day for her.

—⁓—

One year at a women's retreat, I was in charge of the craft session. I had shopped, gathered, and created packets for each woman, then put them in a box. But, unbeknownst to me, I left the box by the front door. At 11 P.M. my husband and children showed up at the retreat center, miles and miles away, with the craft box so I wouldn't be embarrassed by my mistake.

Jackie Rhoden, Vista

What a stupid thing to say! I couldn't believe I said it. As the words were tumbling out of my mouth, I could see myself trying to reel them back in. But just like a big game fish, the phrase kept pulling line and sinking my well-being. After saying this I felt like I could have walked under the door without ever opening it. And the worst part is, there was nothing that could possibly make up for what I said.

This is embarrassing when it happens with strangers, but it can be devastating when it happens with your wife. You forget her birthday. You overlook your anniversary. You make a comment at a party about how, when she is really tired, she snores just like her uncle Don, and everybody has a good laugh at her expense. Can you still feel the frost that blew through your home when you got the icy treatment from your wife?

We've all done it. We have all found some pretty creative ways to talk our way right out of the bedroom and into the dog house. Pam and I were in an intense time of life trying to get her undergraduate degree completed. She was pushing hard, and I was trying to keep up with the added responsibilities of helping around the house so she would have time for her studies. I was becoming overwhelmed with the work load, and we were growing increasingly distant from one another because of the demands of our life.

That's when Pam decided she needed to take drastic measures. She could see the distance that was developing

A Little Extra

If your lover has children from a previous relationship, give each of them a gift that shows your love for her. A ring they each wear, flowers for the girls, or a tee-shirt for the boys will all serve to announce the value you place on her as their mother.

—⚏—

The first time my husband came over to meet my daughter impressed me. He rang the doorbell and my five-year-old daughter answered the door. He extended his arm and held out a beautiful bouquet of flowers for her. He could have been intimidated by the possibility of an instant family, but he started things right and has since captured both of our hearts.

Angela Carmazzi, Sacramento

Encouraging Words

Choose a word your wife uses to demean herself and turn the opposite into a compliment you use often. If she calls herself, "ugly," call her "beautiful." If she calls herself, "dumb," call her, "smart." If she calls herself, "plain," call her "extraordinary."

—⁓—

My husband is a man of few words. When I was pregnant I would ask him, "Do I look fat? Do you love me?"

His answer was always, "No, You look skinny and yes, I love you."

I asked him so many times that one day when I got in my car to go to the store, there on the dash board was a permanent sign that said: Skinny, I love you!

Irene Dorado, Santa Fe Springs

between us, and she wanted to interrupt the cycle. I, on the other hand, was numb and focused on just surviving her last semester. I was not too interested in being in love. She went to the store to find a way to get my attention and found herself walking through the lingerie department looking for new pajamas that would be sure to make me sit up and take notice. With anticipation building in her heart, she joyfully paid for the outfit and headed home, intimate thoughts captivating her imagination. When the kids went to bed that night, Pam made her move. She curled her hair, put on fresh perfume, and got dressed in her new lingerie. She then sauntered out of the bedroom and approached me with that look in her eyes.

I would like to say that I responded admirably, but the fact is, I blew it. I was so wrapped up in my own needs that I was irritated by Pam's attempt. I had allowed my frustration about Pam's schedule to carry my mind away. I was thinking she was selfish and uncaring about me, and in response I had become numb and unfeeling about her. When she walked out in this really cute outfit, I should have been bowled over and had my engine racing. Instead, I nonchalantly looked up from what I was doing with a blank look on my face. I could tell she wanted me to be excited about her, but I was not going to give in. To be perfectly honest, I thought it would be too much work to try to keep up with her and repair the hurt that had built up in our relationship over the past few months.

Well, Pam panicked and ran back to the bedroom in tears. Normally I would have followed her and tried to make up with her, but I didn't want to be the one this time. So I just sat in the living room and went back to what I was doing. I am not sure exactly why I thought this would work, but I was determined not to be the one to give in. Eventually, Pam came out of the bedroom dressed in much different clothes. I had the thought then that I should probably try to mend things with her, but I fought it off for a couple more days.

The Great Escape

Try an unscheduled getaway. Rent a nice hotel room and do what you want when you want. Sleep when you want to sleep. Eat when you want to eat. Shop when, and if, you want to shop. The key is to relax and do what the two of you want to do when you want to do it.

Just the Two of Us

Take your wife back. Go back and relive the day you proposed to her. Remember as much as you can and do it again. Take her to the same places. Ask her again to marry you. Take her to a nice dinner and thank her for saying yes.

Finally I started to return to my senses—I realized that I still had to live with this woman!

So, when you find yourself in hot water, how do you get yourself back into good graces with your wife?

1. Check your attitude. Often the mistakes you make are a result of a bad attitude you have allowed to fester. You are hurt because she has neglected certain needs of yours. You are feeling lonely because you think she is withholding sex from you. You are angry because she has a stronger personality than yours and she overwhelms you when you try to bring up your concerns in life.

Or maybe you are just perturbed because she approaches life differently than you and you are tired of it. She spends money differently than you, she approaches responsibilities in life differently than you, and she does relationships differently than you. Eventually you start thinking she is wrong rather than just different. Ask yourself, "Am I willing to let her back in my heart? Is this really that big of an offense? Is it going to be worth the loneliness and tension to hold on to this conflict?"

2. Seize the opportunities. Your wife wants to have a relationship with you that works. As a result, she will give you opportunities to get back into her good graces—but you have to recognize them. She will probably not walk up to you and say, "Okay, Bozo, I forgive you for the stupid thing you did, but now I am ready to give you a second chance. If you don't blow it this time, we'll call it even."

You might be wondering, "Why can't it be that way? If my wife would be that up front with me, I could probably figure out how to keep her happy."

Well, quit wishing, because it's not likely to happen. Instead, she will give you clues. These clues are opportunities to notice her needs and respond in a gentle and strategic fashion. If you notice the clues and take advantage of the open door, you will see your love grow. If you miss the clues, or refuse to respond to them, then your wife will continue to feel insecure and hesitant to trust you.

Pam gave me two clues. The first was verbal. She passed by me on the second day and said, "So are we ever going to talk about what happened or are you just going to stay out of touch?"

Building Anticipation

Write a letter to your spouse inviting her on your next date or vacation. Tell her the reasons why you are looking forward to spending time with her.

—⁓—

My husband planned a weekend away, arranged child care, then wrote a letter inviting me to come!

Marion Sawatzky, Reedley

Talking It Over

Questions for you: When you have made a mistake
with your wife, do you feel more
embarassed or more inadequate?

When your wife extends forgiveness to you, how does it affect
the way you look at the rest of
your life?

Questions for her: What have I done to try to help
that has gotten in the way?

What have I not done that
you would like me to do to help
you grow?

I didn't like the tone or the content of her question, and
my first inclination was to get angry. It felt a little like I was
being given the chance to sleep on a sheet of ice. I stopped
myself from reacting and decided to think through my
response. I realized that if I talked with her and tried to work
through this, there could be joy waiting at the end of the
rocky trial. I was also completely convinced that if I didn't
talk with her, she could give me the cold-shoulder treatment
for an indefinite period of time. So we talked. It took a few
days of long conversations to convince her that I really did
still love her and was still interested in her sexually.

The second clue came after our days of talking as a test
to see if I meant what I said. I was once again doing some
miscellaneous work around the house one evening when

Pam approached me wearing those same new pajamas. This clue was the critical one. If I failed this one, my wife would boycott being my girlfriend. If I succeeded, however, I would be back on the path together with Pam, and we would both be a lot happier. This time I was smart enough to notice and show my enthusiasm about my wife.

So often at this point, we men somehow come up with the idea that this is a good time to retaliate against our wives by withholding our response. We figure this will help her know how much we are hurt by the bad dynamic we are caught in. This is about as smart as putting sugar in your own gas tank so that no one will have to depend upon you for rides anymore. You punish only yourself when you withhold affection from your wife.

3. *Say, "I'm sorry."* As Pam and I were in the middle of reinstating our passion for one another, it dawned on me, *It*

The Gift of Love

As a gift to your wife, finish something you have started. Thank her when you are done for being so patient with you.

—⁓—

For our first anniversary, my husband presented me with a pile of wood, which was to become a four-poster bed for us. For two years it sat in the garage. Then, for our third anniversary, Brad completed his beautiful work of art by spending weeks of midnights to get it built for our anniversary.

Gina Willems, Bakersfield

The Gift of Love

After an argument when you were wrong, buy your wife a dozen flowers, wrap an apology note around each stem, and deliver them to her.

———

My husband always apologizes after we argue, usually calling from work the next day. One day he didn't call to apologize. So when he got home that night I was really mad. When he came in, he asked, "Did you get the mail?" When I said no, he told me to go get the mail; I stormed out of the house to our mailbox—which was filled with flowers and an apology note.

was pretty stupid of me to distance myself from her. As I was willing to let Pam back in, my heart softened toward her and I began to remember why I married her. I remembered the joy she brought and the way she filled the gaps in my life. I was amazed at how quickly we were able to fall in love again.

As I realized how much I had missed by being upset with Pam, I looked her in the eyes and said, "I am sorry. I am sorry for allowing myself to get so distant from you and for allowing our relationship to suffer."

She melted in my arms. I didn't understand at first why this had such a profound impact on her, but I have come to realize that honesty builds trust when it is shared gently. Your wife is wired for conversation and interrelating. She is probably adept at conversation, and she most likely spends long hours talking with friends. In a word, women are conversational. As a result, transparency comes much easier for her than for you. When you are transparent enough to say you are sorry for the mistakes you make, she concludes you are in touch with reality and worth trusting again.

4. *Make the apology as big as the faux paus*. When Jesse walked in the door from work, his oldest son asked, "What are we going to do for Mom's birthday today?"

Use Your Imagination

Next time you have a disagreement with your wife, think about what it is that is driving you crazy. You may be married to a creative woman whose attention to detail slows down your life. You may be married to an ambitious woman whose incessant ideas makes it hard for you to relax. You may have a dramatic, fun-loving wife whose overreactions shock you. When the argument is over, write your lover a note that points out the characteristic you love that prompted the conflict.

—m—

At times we would be in a tiff with one another. Often I would be in bed when he got home, and he would come and kneel by the bed and ask for forgiveness. We had one of our disagreements when I had been especially difficult. He had to go to work before we could resolve our difference. When he came home that night from a meeting, he said, "You can't out love me." Since then we've had a goal to try to "out love" one another.

Cathy Fellahaum, Bakersfield

The Gift of Love

Give your wife the gift of cuddling. Set aside a night to sit on the couch and snuggle. While you sit close enough to touch one another, listen to your favorite music, review a favorite photo album, read a good book to each other, or watch a movie. Plan on not having sex unless she initiates it.

Jesse had forgotten Sandy's birthday! It was going to be a very bad night. He tried to pull himself together and think of something he could pull off in a hurry but it was too late. Sandy had bounded to the door to see what surprise he was going to have waiting for her. When she realized that her surprise was a brain-dead husband, she was livid.

Jesse disappeared out the door to head to the store. He bought a bakery-made birthday cake, a humorous card, and a bouquet of flowers. He walked through the front door with his hands full of last-minute birthday paraphernalia and his heart full of the pathetic hope that maybe she would overlook his failing. The tension in the air as he arrived told him he was going to be in for a long night. The family faked their way through a birthday dinner. Sandy wouldn't say much as she sat in her chair with her lips pressed together, answering every question with a one word answer. She got up before dinner was over and went to her bedroom. Jesse figured the celebration was over, so he quickly cleaned up the dishes. The kids disappeared to their rooms in case war broke out. Jesse headed out to the garage, figuring Sandy would not want to see him for a while.

When Sandy came out of the bedroom an hour later, she realized that all inhabitable portions of her house had been evacuated. Sandy felt like she had been abandoned on a day that was supposed to be special. Sandy felt anything but special. As she stared at the cake that no one had dared to touch, her mind raced. She carefully took a knife out of the drawer and cut a large piece of her cake, placed it on a plate, and started toward the garage. Jesse whirled around in surprise when he heard the garage door open. He was hoping that Sandy had calmed down.

Sheepishly he said, "Happy birthday, Sandy."

She never smiled. She just coldly said, "Here's your piece of cake," and threw it across the garage. The plate barely missed Jesse's head as it whizzed by his ear and shattered against the wall. Jesse looked back to see the piece of cake

Talking It Over

Questions for you:
Think back to the last time your wife accepted an apology from you. Did you say, "Thank you?" If not, take time now and tell her how much you appreciate her forgiveness.

Questions for her:
What area of your life are you trying to make changes in right now?

What areas of life do you struggle with most?

stuck to the wall, hovering over the broken evidence of Sandy's temper.

Jesse snapped. They spent the next two hours yelling and screaming at each other. They never did figure out how this fight got so out of hand. They were both hurt and were taking it out on each other. Either of them could have softened the situation, but they both let their anger get out of control.

After a lonely night on the couch, Jesse went to work mulling over the night before. He realized that he had blown it. He thought Sandy was wrong for sending cake into orbit and flying off the handle, but he was willing to admit his own thoughtlessness started it. He had a hard time concentrating on work, so he decided to take the afternoon off and get a plan together.

Jesse remembered a Bed and Breakfast not far from home that Sandy had been talking about for months. He made reservations and had a certificate made up. He bought a dozen roses to display the gift certificate, then headed toward home. On the way he stopped at a fabric store and bought a small piece of white fabric. He also found a stick and tied the fabric to the top.

Jesse walked to the front door, rang the doorbell, then walked in flag first. Sandy was in the back of the house and saw the flag at the end of the hallway as she headed toward the ringing of the bell. She was taken back that Jesse was pleading surrender, but wasn't sure she wanted to let him off the hook just for a white flag. Jesse peered around the corner and assessed the safety of the situation. When the flowers came into Sandy's view, Jesse noticed a tinge of interest on her part.

He held the flowers out and said, "I am sorry about last night. I blew it. If I could do last night again, I would sure do it differently. I know this won't make up for last night, but if you can find it in your heart to forgive me, I would like to try again."

Sandy reluctantly accepted the flowers and then noticed the gift certificate. In her heart she thought, *It's a good thing there's more than flowers because he has a lot of ground to make up.*

A Little Extra

Show your wife she is valued by honoring her past. Rather than being insecure about the role other people have played in her life, honor the positive effects of her relationship with an ex-husband, her parents, or a close friend. A handmade craft that commemorates one of these relationships will be treasured for the rest of her life.

—⟋⟍—

One day, my husband Mark carved I love you in our kitchen cutting board. Years later, Mark became ill with cancer and passed away. Steve, a good single friend to Mark and I, kept in contact with the kids and me to see how we were doing. Steve was a part of our small group Bible study, too. Eventually we fell in love and were married. Steve was good to keep Mark in conversations with the kids. He never felt like he had to compete with Mark. One year for Christmas, after a move to a new house, I opened up a gift. Inside was the cutting board with the I love you that Mark had carved. Steve had added photos of Mark with the kids and I, and had it made into a beautiful wall hanging.

Denise Redden, Vista

It was wise that Jesse had made the reservations for two weeks ahead because it was going to take a few days for Sandy to refocus her emotions to include Jesse. But as she dwelled upon the effort and forethought her husband had invested in his apology, she slowly grew interested. As the reality of spending two days at a Victorian Bed and Breakfast came into focus, she decided she did not want to spend time at a nice hotel while she was mad. Sandy forgave her husband's failure, and they had a wonderful mini-vacation together.

When you mess up small, a small apology will do fine. But when you have taken a major fall, you need to call 911 and take emergency measures. The key is to make sure the effort of the apology matches the intensity of the offense.

7

Exploring the Mystery of Your Wife

With you there is life and joy and peace and all good things—away from you there is turmoil and anguish and blank despair.

—BERTRAND RUSSELL

I t is obvious to me that we will never fully understand our wives. The best we can do is to keep learning. We can begin the process of discovering who they are by having them tell us over and over again what motivates them and what beats in their hearts.

One of the most important things I ever learned in life is to ask good questions and then listen to the answers. This can be quite a challenge to most men, because our wives don't communicate with us the way we listen. We listen like a waffle and she talks like spaghetti. As men, we have a tendency to ask questions that will bring us predictable answers. That way we don't have to work too hard at listening. Our wives, however, like to keep conversations fluid and dynamic. They can change subjects on you as often as spaghetti intersects. You

---

❧ *How to Pick Up Your Wife:* I want to get lost inside of you.

Talking It Over

Questions for you: How does it help you that your wife is good at starting conversations?

What is your greatest emotional fear with your wife—that she will find you uninteresting over time? that she will think you are shallow? that she will make loving her too complicated? that you will never figure her out?

Questions for her: What is the most significant spiritual experience you have had?

What emotional words do you associate with our relationship right now?

may find it exasperating to try and keep up with her as she journeys through her conversations with you. You may even feel like something terribly wrong has happened in your life. You got married because you were convinced you and your wife would have an experience filled with good times, and now you are wondering if some virus has invaded your relationship and reprogrammed your wife to drive you nuts.

So how do you keep intimacy viruses from infecting your relationship?

First, *take turns in communication*. When it is your turn to talk, you are going to want to stay on subject. Most men approach conversations as if they are problem solving. We will introduce the subject, explore the possibilities, and make a decision. That's why we love sports, computers, and projects. We can focus, get lost in the experience, and not complicate things by bringing in a bunch of peripheral thoughts.

The tendency I see among men is avoidance of conversation because we feel inadequate. Our wives' ability to move from one subject to another can make us feel shallow and clumsy. We look to the women in our lives in utter amazement at the volume of words and flexibility of conversation they are able to effortlessly engage in. This makes us feel like we are lagging behind and in need of intense training before we will be mature conversationalists. The truth,

The Gift of Love

The greatest gift you can give your lover is commitment. Tell your wife often that you are in the race to win, that you will never leave her or forsake her.

—⁓—

I come from a family with a history of over fifty divorces. My husband's parents just celebrated sixty-two years together. Thirty-three years ago, when we were first married, I said something sharp to him. He sensed my insecurity and said, "There is nothing you can do to make me quit loving you!" I suddenly realized I had been trying to make him quit loving me so the pain would be over sooner. His words cemented my trust in him!

Jan Arensmier, Madera

A Little Extra

Choose a phrase you will repeat often that expresses to your lover how much better your life is with her. Phrases such as, "I am the luckiest man on earth," "My life is brighter since you brought your sunshine my way," "You are the best thing that ever happened to me," and "I am more myself when I am with you than at any other time" are especially effective.

—⁓—

After 27 years he still says, "You are prettier than the day I married you. You are so great to keep hanging in there with all these projects I keep trying. I am the luckiest man in the world. I could never have found anyone better than you!"

Mary Lynn, Saugus

however, is that we communicate in a different way. Her way of communicating is not *better* than yours, just different.

Pay attention to details. Women, on the other hand, like to integrate numerous thoughts into one conversation. She is wired to take verbal journeys. When she has the freedom to visit many areas of her life with you in conversation, she feels a deeper connection to you. She feels you are treating her life as if it is a priceless treasure you hold in your hands. When you encourage her to talk by actively listening, she finds you more attractive and she becomes more confident in loving you. It is not natural for most men to take this journey in their interactions, so it may seem a waste of time at first. But it is in your best interests to see this as an *investment*.

Your wife will become more interesting to you as you discover more about her, and you will become more interesting to her as she senses your interest in the details of her life.

Ask lots of questions: Your wife will be convinced you are interested in her if you are actively pursuing conversation with her. The trend of life is to limit our conversations to the responsibilities of life. It takes little or no effort to recognize the need to talk about bills, the kids, schedules, and demands. If all you dwell on as a couple, however, is the demands of your life, you will find yourselves demanding a better life. To keep your romantic interest alive, you will need to deliberately think of questions to ask that will focus the conversation on intimate, interesting, and insightful topics. Start with the

Memories

Use pictures from your wedding to make a memento for your wife.

—⁂—

Greg wanted me to always remember him as the romantic man I fell in love with. He had an enlargement of our engagement picture made and framed it in a beautiful wooden frame. In the glass cover he had etched the Bible verse that most reminds him of me. Now, every time I walk past our engagement picture, I am reminded of my worth to Greg. Etched in the glass are the words, "Her worth is far above jewels. The heart of her husband trusts in her" (Proverbs 31:10-11).

Kathy Matis, San Marcos

From Pam's Heart

On our fourth anniversary, I was two weeks from delivering our first baby, and I was HUGE! And I felt huge! I was in no mood for what couples usually do on anniversaries! Bill cooked a lavish candlelight dinner, and then handed me a gift in a HUGE box! As I unwrapped it, I began to laugh. Inside was a food processor, pajamas for nursing days ahead, and a board game for us to play. Nothing sexy in the box—and I loved Bill for it! Every year before I had wanted the usual: jewels, sexy clothing, or very romantic treasures. But sometimes the best gift is no pressure!

questions in this chapter, then write down questions as they come to mind.

Make eye contact: If you say you want to listen to your wife but your eyes are wandering, you will catch a full share of grief. Look into her eyes and show her you are genuinely interested. Practice this skill until it becomes a habit for you.

Participate in the journey: Your wife does not want to talk to a statue and she does not want to be interrogated. She wants to have interactive, variegated talks with you. Ask her clarifying questions that keep her talking. Recap her thoughts in your own words and ask her, "Is that what you meant?" Most of all, don't try to fix her when she is traveling through her thoughts. If you resort to being her mechanic, you will never be invited into the front seat—or the back seat for that matter!

When you have won your wife's heart, the payoff is marvelous. After years of romancing Pam, she presented me with the following poem:

THE WINNER

No contest!
No holds barred!
Hands down,
Through the goal posts,
Out of the ball park,
Nothing but net,
Checkered flag,
Gold medal,
Got my heart,
Winner!

When she presented me with this gift, I definitely felt like a winner!

From Pam's Heart

Bill has looked for ways of encouraging me as a way of life, using simple sentences sprinkled throughout our tightly scheduled days. When I am running errands and I have to stop by home or the office for something quickly, I usually shout out, "Just me!" Bill's response is always "Not just you—*especially* you!"

And on those especially hectic days when the stress of life seems to be weighing heavy on our shoulders, Bill will reach out, take my hand, and say, "I'd rather be busy with you than have an easier life with anyone else."

Talking It Over

Questions for you:

Finish this statement: When I am romantically consumed with you, I am desperate? . . . focused? . . . intrigued? . . . fascinated?

How do you feel when your wife makes romantic overtures toward you?

Questions for her:

Describe to me the connection inside you between romance and sex.

What do you think about when we have sex?

When you get aroused, where does it start in your body? How does it progress?

What gets you in the mood?

Let Her Know You Love Her

Stand in front of your wife and tell her everything you like about her. You get extra points if she is not wearing clothes and you compliment parts of her body she does not expect you to find attractive. With a twinkle in your eye, tell her that you do not know these details about any other woman.

—ᴡᴡ—

Every morning my husband brings me coffee as I step out of the shower. One morning he commented how glad he was that we were married and sexually there for each other. He was fully clothed and I was standing there naked. After two children and several added rolls during our forty-five years together, his words made me feel warm and tingly!

Michele Coutts, San Ramon

CREATING ROMANTIC
MOMENTS TOGETHER

BILL & PAM FARREL

*A*dd sparkle and fun to your relationship
with these recipes for romance and one-
of-a-kind activities for couples in love.
From original romantic traditions to easy-
to-plan dates, *Love to Love You* is filled
with scores of imaginative ideas.

*Discover the joy of creative romance—
Come together heart to heart!*